Learn
Markdown

The Complete Guide on Markdown Formatting

By

Khurshid Alam

LEAF PRESS

Copyright © 2018 Khurshid Alam

All Rights Reserved.

No part of this book may be reproduced, stored in a retrieval system, or transmitted by any means, electronic, mechanical, photocopying, recording or otherwise without written permission from the copyright holder.

First Edition, April 2018

KDP ISBN: 9781980616498

CCM ISBN: 9788193554302 (ebook)

CCM ISBN: 9788193554319 (paperback)

Published and Distributed by
Creative Content Media (Leaf Press)
605, Classic Exotica, Kondhwa Khurd
Pune 411048, Maharashtra, India.
Email" leafpress.ccm@gmail.com
http://www.leafpress.in
Mob: +91-87938-82210

To my mother

Sayida Khatoon

About the author

Khurshid Alam, MA in English, works as a team lead in technical documentation department with an IT company based in Pune, Maharashtra (India). He has more than 12 years' experience in documentation, having worked on almost all types of documents including user guide, admin guide, installation guide, Help, case studies, brochures, white papers, product sheets, and more.

He designs templates for various sets of technical documents and Help tools, follows globally recognized style guides such as Microsoft Technical Publication (MSTP) and Apple Style Guide, has written an in-house style guide to be followed by other writers, has written *A Guide on Usage of Terminologies for Documentation and Software Applications* targeted to be used by user interface (UI) teams, developers, and other writers to maintain consistency in terminologies for various products.

He edits documents written by other writers and trains them on various authoring tools such as Microsoft Word, Adobe Acrobat Prof Editor, Microsoft Expression Web, HTML Help Workshop, Markdown Editor, Adobe RoboHelp, Adobe FrameMaker, Adobe Captivate, PPT, SnagIT, Microsoft Visio, Microsoft Visual SourceSafe (VSS), and Concurrent Versions System (CVS).

Besides, he has more than 100 of poems, several stories, research papers, and two books including *Investigative Poetry & Other Poems* (ISBN-13: 978-1499755718) published to his credit.

Foreword

There are several Markdown editors or tools, including that of the GitHub Flavored Markdown (GFM) ones. In this book, I have added the syntaxes available in most of the tools to give you a complete guide on Markdown editing with a focus not to miss out even a single syntax. You can simply use these syntaxes to reflect the desired result in the tools you use. In some tools, you may find predefined styles for all the syntaxes; you simply need to apply them. But one thing is certain that in all the tools you can affect the formatting by using any syntax.

The best thing is that if you need to add certain things and you don't find any syntax for that in your Markdown editor, or there is no syntax for a style, you can simply use normal HTML tags (markup codes for HTML). That will work fine. All Markdown editor is markup codes compliant.

The basic logic behind Markdown is to format the HTML document is an easier way and as there are no tags to use the output, it is very light in size.

If you find anything more should be added, please feel free to write to scripting4u@yahoo.com.

Khurshid Alam

Pune, India.

Table of Contents

Introducing Markdown 12

   What is Markdown? 12

   Markdown: History 12

   Markdown: Usability 13

Learn Markdown Syntax 16

   Headings 16

      Changing heading level 17

   Body Text 18

      Regular font type 18

      Italics font type (emphasis) 18

      Bold font type (strong emphasis) 19

      Bold and italics font type 19

   Indentation 20

   Strikethrough 21

   Underline 21

   Horizontal Line 22

   Lists 23

      Ordered List 23

      Unordered List 27

      Task List 30

   Table 32

   Comments 34

   Quotes or Block 35

   Text Highlighting 38

   Code Block 39

   Inline Code 40

   Code Fences 41

- Footnotes 42
- Link References 43
  - *Backlink* *43*
  - *Use URL* *44*
  - *Link for emails* *45*
- Title attribute 45
- Anchors 46
- Images 47
  - *Reference link* *47*
  - *Inline link* *47*
- Videos 47
- Embedding HTML 48
- Copyright 49
- Emoji 49
- Escaping 51
- Keyboard keys 53
- Custom Themes 54
- Table of Contents 54

Learn Keyboard Shortcuts for Syntax 58

What is Markdown?

Introducing Markdown

Before you start working in Markdown, you should be familiar with it.

What is Markdown?

Markdown, contrary to the markup language, is a plain text formatting method. Formatting is done in structured style using syntax, which is basically punctuations and characters. In Markdown, you don't need to create any styles for formatting; either your editor has a predefined style for formatting that you can apply or you can type a syntax directly to reflect the formatting. In case, you don't find any syntax for formatting, you can simply use the tags that you may use in normal HTML.

> *"Markdown is a text-to-HTML conversion tool for web writers. Markdown allows you to write using an easy-to-read, easy-to-write plain text format, then convert it to structurally valid XHTML (or HTML)."*
>
> *— John Gruber, Daring Fireball*

Markdown: History

John Gruber devised the syntax-based formatting in 2004 to avoid using HTML tags. Gruber preferred the style as raw but it soon became preferred by web writers, given its simple applicability. The first Markdown editor by Gruber was written in Perl.

Markdown: Usability

Markdown is a lightweight plain text file and is best preferred for the web-based content, standalone web pages, and single HTML pages such as readme, user license, privacy policy, terms & conditions, FAQs, email text, discussion forums, blogs, and others. Most of the blogging platforms have plugins for Markdown. Github uses Markdown widely for formatting the documents. Markdown also gives good result for the Help files for handheld devices and HTML5.

In Markdown, the document is formatted in a single source and can be easily converted to multiple formats including HTML, Word, PDF, other outputs based on the tools you use. Most of the common file extensions of Markdown files are `.md` or `.markdown`.

There are several tools, especially web-based, that display the syntax codes and the result in two panes side-by-side, very much similar when you compare two documents in Microsoft Word. This helps in understanding how the result would be, as you go on formatting.

Markdown Syntax

Learn Markdown Syntax

In Markdown, formatting syntax is explicitly written that makes it very simple to understand and use.

Headings

For headings, use hash symbol (#) before the text that you want to display as heading.

You may add hash symbol at the end but you do not require to match the number of hashes with the beginning hashes.

- Use one hash symbol (#) for heading level 1 <h1>,
- Use two hash symbols (##) for heading level 2 <h2>, and
- Follow this pattern up to heading level 6.

In Markdown, you can use up to heading level 6. However, using heading level up to 3 or 4 would be enough.

Example:

Syntax	Result
#Heading 1# or type the equal signs under the heading like Heading 1 =========	**Heading 1**

##Heading 2# or type dashes under the heading like Heading 2 --------------	**Heading 2**
###Heading 3###	**Heading 3**
####Heading 4####	**Heading 4**
#####Heading 5#####	**Heading 5**
######Heading 6######	**Heading 6**

Note: The hashes at the beginning matter and not at the end. Adding closing hashes is irrelevant.

Changing heading level

Sometimes you may need to change the heading level, from bigger to smaller (`<h1>` to `<h2>`) or vice verse. You can change the heading level in any of the following ways.

- Markdown style: In most of the desktop Markdown tools, you will find the formatting option for this, termed as Increase Heading Level and Decrease Heading Level. You can apply this option for changing the heading level.

- Syntax: You can also type the shortcut for syntax as `Ctrl + =` to increase the heading level or `Ctrl + -` to decrease the heading level.

Body Text

You can use regular font type for your paragraph. For space before and after the lines, you can customize the template that you wish to use. Moreover, you can give extra breaks between paragraphs by pressing the Enter key.

However, you cannot indent paragraphs with tab or space.

For body text, you can use the following font types.

Regular font type

For formatting regular font type, you do not need any syntax. Actually, your tool, in which you work, will determine the regular font type. The entire body text will accept the same formatting style.

However, you can customize the template to change the font type, font size, font color, before and after spaces of each paragraph or other such elements in the CSS file. For that, check whether your Markdown editor allows to do so.

Importantly, you cannot apply different font types to different paragraphs as you do in a Microsoft Word document.

Also, don't indent your paragraph with spaces or tabs. Markdown will not reflect such indentation.

Italics font type (emphasis)

To display a heading, title, section, or paraphrases, you may use italics font type.

Use one star mark (*) or an underscore (_) before and after the paraphrases.

Example:

Syntax	Result
Title	*Title*
Title	*Title*

Note the placement of the marks.

Bold font type (strong emphasis)

To display a heading, title, section, or paraphrases, you may use bold font type.

Use two star marks (**) or two underscores (_ _) before and after the paraphrases.

Example:

Syntax	Result
Title	**Title**
__Title__	**Title**

Bold and italics font type

To display a heading, title, section, or paraphrases, you may use both bold and italics font type.

Use three star marks (*****), or three underscores (**_ _ _**), or a combination of one star mark and two underscores (***_ _**), or one underscore and two star marks (**_****) before and after the paraphrases.

Example:

Syntax	Result
Title	*Title*
___Title___	*Title*
__Title__	*Title*
**Title**	*Title*

Indentation

In Markdown, you can indent a list and not a paragraph. You can change the indentation of a list in any of the following ways.

- Markdown style: In most of the desktop Markdown editors, you will find an option to change the indentation (indent, outdent) for the list. Select the list and apply the option.
- Syntax: You may also type a keyboard shortcut `Ctrl + ]` to increase the indentation or `Ctrl + [` to decrease the indentation.

Strikethrough

To strike through the terms in the body text, you may use any of the following ways.

- Markdown style: In most of the desktop Markdown editors, you will find the formatting style for it. Select the term and apply that formatting to it.
- Syntax: Type two tilde marks (~~) around the term.

Example:

Syntax	Result
~~strike through~~	~~strike through~~

Underline

To underline the terms in the body text, you may use any of the following ways.

- Markdown style: In most of the desktop Markdown editors, you will find the formatting style for it. Select the term and apply that formatting to it.
- Syntax: Embrace the terms with <u> and </u>.

Example:

Syntax
<u>There is a man standing over there.</u>

Result

<u>There is a man standing over there.</u>

Horizontal Line

You may need to divide the content body into sections. In Markdown, you can do so by giving a horizontal line in any of the following ways.

- Markdown style: In many of the desktop Markdown editors, you will find an option to place a horizontal line. You can apply this option.

- Syntax: You can also type three or more dashes (---), underscores (_ _ _), or asterisks (***) without spaces in between as syntax to place the horizontal line and then press the Enter key.

Example:

Syntax

This is how you can place a horizontal line to separate content body into sections.

Result

This is how you can place a horizontal line to separate content body into sections.

Lists

There are two types of lists, ordered or numbered list and unordered or bulleted list.

Ordered List

If you want to number your list, use Ordered List that begins with numbering.

In Markdown, the number list always starts from 1 in a series. You cannot restart the numbering order without breaking the series. To break the series, you need to increase the indent of the listing paragraph. Also, the number will always be written in ordinal numbers (1, 2, 3, ...) and not in Roman numbers (i, ii, iii, ...) or alphabets (a, b, c, ...).

For Ordered List, there is no syntax as such but you can number your list in either of the following ways.

- Markdown style: In most of the desktop Markdown tools, you will find the formatting option termed as Ordered List. Select the list and then apply the formatting option in the Markdown tool that you use.

- Syntax: Type 1, give a period (•), and press the space bar on your keyboard. The first item will be numbered and the following items will inherit the numbering style in sequence.

Example:

Ordered list	Result
1. Item 1	1. Item 1
2. Item 2	2. Item 2
3. Item 3	3. Item 3
4. Item 4 and so on	4. Item 4 and so on

If you type 1. followed by a space to each item in the list, all the items will be automatically numbered in sequence.

Example:

Ordered list	Result
1. Item 1	1. Item 1
1. Item 2	2. Item 2
1. Item 3	3. Item 3
1. Item 4 and so on	4. Item 4 and so on

Sublist

You can use sublist or nested list within your list in the following way.

- Select the list within the numbered list and then increase the indent with the Markdown option or press Tab on your keyboard. The selected list will restart the list.

Example:

Sublist in an ordered list

1. Item 1
2. Item 2
   1. Item 3
   2. Item 4
3. Item 5
4. Item 6

Note that the nested list always starts from 1 in ordinal number.

Unordered List in Ordered List

You can also use an Unordered List in an Ordered List in the following ways.

1. Select the list within the numbered list and then increase the indent. The selected list will restart the list.

2. Apply the Unordered List formatting option in the Markdown tool that you use. Or, remove the number and type one of the characters from *, +, - and then press the space bar on your keyboard.

Example:

Syntax	Result

1. Item 1
2. Item 2
   * Item 3
   * Item 4
3. Item 5
4. Item 6
	1. Item 1
	2. Item 2
	   - Item 3
	   - Item 4
	3. Item 5
	4. Item 6

Multiple paragraphs

You may use multiple paragraphs, some with listing and some without.

Type the number 1, give a period (.), and start your paragraph. Press Enter to break the line. The new line will inherit the numbering style.

Press Backspace on the line for which you do not want numbering. This will remove the numbering. Repeat this for the next lines.

Example:

1. This is a paragraph. This paragraph is numbered.

   This paragraph is in continuation with the previous one without numbering.

2. This paragraph is numbered.

> This paragraph is without numbering.

3. This paragraph is also numbered.

Block in a list

You may list your paragraphs and insert blocks.

Example:

Syntax

* You can create a list item and then place the blocks like this.

    > This is the block.

    > This is also the block.

* The list continues.

Result

- You can create a list item and then place the blocks like this.

    > This is the block.
    >
    > This is also the block.

- The list continues.

Unordered List

In most of the desktop Markdown tools, you will find the formatting option for this, termed as Unordered List. You can apply this option for listing.

The bullet list can be created up to any levels, with three different bullet styles: filled circle (•), empty circle (◦), and filled square (■). However, it is advisable to use 3-4 bullet levels.

To change the levels, you need to increase the indent of the listing paragraph.

Unordered List: level 1

For Unordered List, use any of the following syntax for level 1 bullet.

asterisk (*)

At the beginning of the list, type one asterisk symbol (*) and press the space bar on your keyboard.

plus (+)

At the beginning of the list, type one plus symbol (+) and press the space bar on your keyboard.

hyphen (-)

At the beginning of the list, type one hyphen (-) and press the space bar on your keyboard.

Example:

Syntax	Result
* Item 1	• Item 1
+ Item 1	• Item 1

| - Item 1 | • Item 1 |

Unordered List: level 2 and more

You can use sublist or create nested list within your Unordered List.

List the points and then select the lists for which you want to change the level. Increase the indent, the bullet style will automatically change. Repeat this until the level you desire.

Example:

Sublist in an unordered list

- Item 1
- Item 1
- Item 1
    - Item 1
    - Item 1
    - Item 1
        - Item 1
        - Item 1
        - Item 1

You can also type double bullets to a single item in the list, although this is not a preferred listing style.

Type any combination of two characters (asterisk, plus, or hyphen) together and then list your item.

Example:

Double bullets in an unordered list

You can create a list with double bullets to one item.

- Item 1A
- Item 1B
  - Item 2A
  - Item 2B
    - Item 3A
    - Item 3B
      - Item 4A
      - Item 4B

Task List

Task list is the list of the tasks that you want to carry out. Task list is created with a check box before the list. Task may be either complete with a tick-marked check box or incomplete without a tick-marked check box.

You can create the task list in either of the following ways.

- Markdown style: In a desktop Markdown tool, you will find the option for this formatting termed as Task List. Select the list and then apply the required style from the tool that you use. Once you apply the formatting, you can further change the Task Status as complete by clicking the check box or leave it unchecked to show incomplete.

- Syntax: Type a hyphen and an empty square bracket – [ ] for incomplete task or type a hyphen and a square bracket with a cross symbol in the bracket – [x] for complete task at the beginning of the list.

Example:

Syntax	Result
Here goes your task list.	Here goes your task list.
- [x] Wake up.	☑ Wake up.
- [x] Go to wash room.	☑ Go to wash room.
- [x] Brush your teeth.	☑ Brush your teeth.
- [x] Wash your mouth.	☑ Wash your mouth.
- [x] Take exercise.	☑ Take exercise.
- [ ] Have a light breakfast.	☐ Have a light breakfast.
- [ ] Take a bath.	☐ Take a bath.
- [ ] Get ready for office.	☐ Get ready for office.

Table

You may need to present your information in tables. To create a table in Markdown, you can use any of the following ways.

- Markdown style: In most of the desktop Markdown tools, you will find the formatting option for this, termed as Table. You can place the table anywhere you prefer. You can also press the shortcut `Ctrl + T` for table.
- Syntax: (1) In the first row, write the terms for your first column, type a pipe (|), write the terms for your next columns and then press the Enter key. (2) Type two dashes (--), type a pipe, type two dashes again and then press the Enter key.

   Continue the first step for next rows. You may add as many rows and columns as you want.

   In some tools, you may need to add the pipe at the beginning of the first row also. Example: |--|--|

> Note: Even one dash is enough to create the table but Markdown may get confused as one dash is used for bullet list (unordered list). It is advisable to give at least two dashes.

Example:

Syntax

Here is the list for the hours John worked on the same task for three days.

Monday | Tuesday | Wednesday

-- | -- | --

2 hours | 1 hour | 2 hours

3 hours | 2 hours | 2 hours

1 hour | 3 hours | 1 hour

2 hours | 1 hour | 2 hours

0.30 hour | 1 hour | 1 hour

Result

Here is the list for the hours John worked on the same task for three days.

Monday	Tuesday	Wednesday
2 hours	1 hour	2 hours
3 hours	2 hours	2 hours
1 hour	3 hours	1 hour
2 hours	1 hour	2 hours
0.30 hour	1 hour	1 hour

In GitHub Flavored Markdown, you can write the syntax with or without the opening and closing dashes:

| Monday | Tuesday | Wednesday |

|--: |:--:|--:|

| 2 hours | 1 hour | 2 hours |

Adding a colon to the right of the dashes will allow you to right-align the text in the table.

Example:

Syntax

| Monday | Tuesday | Wednesday |

| ------:| -----------:| -----------:|

| 2 hours | 1 hour | 2 hours |

| 3 hours | 2 hours | 2 hours |

Result

Monday	Tuesday	Wednesday
2 hours	1 hour	2 hours
3 hours	2 hours	2 hours

Comments

To write comments, add four spaces before the text.

Example:

Syntax	Result
....Here·runs·your·comment.	Here runs your comment.

Quotes or Block

You may need to change a paragraph or some lines to block or quote. To change the lines to block, use any of the following ways.

- Markdown style: In many of the desktop Markdown editors, you will find an option to change the selected lines to block termed as Quote or Block. You can apply this option for block.
- Syntax: You may also type a greater than sign (>) before the selected lines as the syntax.

Example:

Syntax

> This is how you can change a paragraph to block.

Result

> This is how you can change a paragraph to block.

You can create nested block quotes by using the greater than signs in the following ways.

Example 1:

Syntax

> This is how you can change a paragraph to block.
>
> > This is the indented block paragraph.
>
> This is the continued paragraph in block.

Result

> This is how you can change a paragraph to block.
> > This is the indented block paragraph.
>
> This is the continued paragraph in block.

Example 2:

Syntax

> This is how you can change a paragraph to block.
> > This is the indented block paragraph.
> This is the continued paragraph in block.

Result

> This is how you can change a paragraph to block.
>
> > This is the indented block paragraph.
> > This is the continued paragraph in block.

Similarly, you can add several other elements such as headings, listed items, or comments in the block quotes.

Example:

Syntax

> ## This is the header 2.

>

> 1. Item 1.

> 2. Item 2.

> 3. Item 3.

>

> The paragraph continues here.

Result

> **This is the header 2.**
>
> 1. Item 1.
> 2. Item 2.
> 3. Item 3.
>
> The paragraph continues here.

Text Highlighting

You can highlight your text in the following way.

Type two equal signs (==) before and after the text.

Example:

Syntax	Result
==Highlighted text appears in color==	Highlighted text appears in color

In GitHub Flavored Markdown, you can highlight your comment in color.

Type two backticks (``) around your comment.

Example:

Syntax

```
``
You can highlight your comment this way.
``
```

Result

```
You can highlight your comment this way.
```

Code Block

You can create a code block to highlight the information in a block.

Place a tab or give four spaces. The text will automatically appear in a block.

Example:

Syntax

```
    Block Code
        Block Code
    Block Code
```

Result

```
Block Code
    Block Code
Block Code
```

Inline Code

Inline codes are generally used to highlight some especial information in a single box in a single line. Typically, this box is different from the one used in Code Fences. In some tools, the inline code may appear in color.

You can type the following syntax: type one grave accent or backtick (`` ` ``), type your information, and then type one grave accent again as closing code.

Example:

Syntax

`` `$ 100 x 100 = $ 10,000` ``

Result

`$ 100 x 100 = $ 10,000`

Code Fences

Code fences are generally used to highlight programming language codes or some especial information in a single box.

- Markdown style: In most of the desktop Markdown tools, you will find the formatting option for this, termed as Code Fences or so. You can apply this option
- Syntax: You can also type the following syntax: type three grave accents (```), sh, press the Enter key, type your information, and then type three grave accents again as closing code.

Example:

Syntax

```sh
$ 100 x 100 = $ 10,000
```

Result

```
$ 100 x 100 = $ 10,000
```

Note: Information is suggestive.

Footnotes

If your body text has some footnotes, where you insert explanation to certain terms, you can format your footnotes in the Markdown editor in the following way.

In the sentence, place the curser at the end of the term and type [^1]. If you have more than one note, you can add this syntax with increasing number.

When you finish inserting the syntax, enter the explanatory notes as:

[^1]: Explain your note here.

[^2]: Explain your note here.

Example:

Syntax

When you are entering the green zone, remember you don't carry plastic bottles[^1] and plastic bags[^2].

[^1]: Plastic bottles are not allowed.

[^2]: Plastic carry bags are not allowed.

Result

When you are entering the green zone, remember you don't carry plastic bottles[1] and plastic bags[2].

Link References

You can insert links in Markdown editor anywhere you prefer in two different ways.

Backlink

Link a reference to a URL

To insert a hyperlink, type a square bracket [] followed by a parenthesis (). Type the text in the square bracket and type the hyperlink in the parenthesis.

Example:

Syntax	Result
[Test link](http://testsite.com)	Test link

Link a URL with quotes in the parenthesis that works as a reference identification.

Example:

Syntax	Result
[Test link](http://testsite.com/ "Add text here")	Test link

Create a relative path to the link

Type a square bracket [] and then a parenthesis (). Embrace the text with a slash (/).

Example:

Syntax	Result
[Test link](/Add text here/)	Test link

The text in the square bracket in these cases will be visible on the document with a backlink.

The link will open in the same window.

Use URL

Insert the hyperlink directly in the document wherever you prefer. In this case, remember to begin all the URLs with http://.

The link will open in a new window.

Example:

http://testsite.com

http://www.testsite.com

> Note: Never omit "http://" from any URL.

Alternatively, you can embrace an URL with angular brackets.

Example:

Syntax	Result
<http://testsite.com>	Test site

Link for emails

Type an angular bracket <>, type your email address, type the angular bracket again as a closing code.

Example:

Syntax	Result
<testmail@abc.com>	testmail@abc.com

Title attribute

Attribute is a reference to a hyperlink. When you create a hyperlink, you can add an attribute to the URL. This will help you track your source. You may add the attribute to all URLs you use in your document.

Example:

Syntax

[Hyperlink](https://en.wikipedia.org/wiki/Hyperlink "Wikipedia: Hyperlink")

Result

Hyperlink

Anchors

Anchor link is created to help the readers jump directly to the destination to refer to the relevant information. In Markdown, you can use this anchor to create table of contents, citation, cross-references, and internal links in the same document.

Type a square bracket [] followed by a parenthesis (). In the parenthesis, prefix the tag with a hash mark (#).

Example:

Syntax	Result
[Chapter 1](#chapter1)	Chapter 1
[Chapter 2](#chapter2)	Chapter 2
[Chapter 3](#chapter3)	Chapter 3

The tag in the square bracket is the reference, while the tag in the parenthesis is the destination.

Note the space with the hash symbol.

Images

You can insert images in a Markdown editor anywhere you prefer in two different ways.

Reference link

Type an exclamatory mark (!), a square bracket [], and then a parenthesis (). Type some text in the square bracket and type the path to the image in the parenthesis.

Example:

![Sample image](F:\Docs\Markdown\download1.png)

Inline link

Alternatively, you can simply drag an image to the Markdown editor if it allows. Or, you can use the option given in the Markdown editor you are using.

Example:

![Sample image](http://sampleimage/123.jpg)

Videos

You can add a video in the Markdown file in the following way.

Type an exclamatory mark (!), a square bracket [], and then two parentheses ()() without space in between.

Type some text in the square bracket and type the link to the image for the video in the first parenthesis and then type the link to the video in the second parenthesis.

Example:

![Sample image](https://link to image of the video)(https://link to the video)

> In Markdown, video must be displayed through the image.

Embedding HTML

Whenever required, you can place HTML code in your Markdown document. This will work similarly as it works in HTML pages.

For example, if you want to add a clickable button, you can place its code.

Example:

Syntax

<button class="button">Click Button</button>

Result

[Click Button]

Copyright

To indicate copyright, type the following syntax.

Example:

Syntax	Result
&copy;	©

Emoji

Emoji emoticons are used to express various emotions. There are hundreds of Emoji emoticons that you can use in Markdown.

Embrace an emoticon with colons. However, you need to check which Emoji emoticon is supported in your Markdown editor.

Example: Type a colon (:), type the term for Emoji emoticon, and then type the colon again.

Most of the desktop Markdown editors will show you a list of several related emoticons that you can select from.

If you have to use more than one word, add the words with underscore to make them one term.

Example:

Examples of emoticons

Other examples:

Syntax	Result
:angry:	😬
:astonished:	😲
:blush:	☺️
:cry:	😢
:frowning:	😦
:innocent:	😇
:kissing:	😗

Syntax	Result
:laughing:	😄
:relaxed:	☺️
:satisfied:	😄
:sleeping:	😪
:smile:	😄
:star:	☆
:wink:	😉

Escaping

In Markdown, a back slash is used to escape undesired formatting.

For example, there may be situations when you would require to show certain terms in star marks (*). However, in Markdown, star marks before the terms would convert them to italics. Luckily, you can escape converting such terms from italics by using a back slash.

Example:

Type a back slash (*back slash*) before and after the term that you mark with stars. This will show the term in star marks without italics.

> Note their placement.

Similarly, if you write an ordinal number, which is not an ordered list and you use a period after that, such text will be converted to ordered list. Add a back slash to avoid converting it to ordered list.

Example:

Syntax

2017\. What a memorable year it was.

Result

2017. What a memorable year it was.

> Note the placement of the back slash.

You can create backslash for any of these characters in Markdown.

Symbols	Markdown characters
Asterisk	*
Backslash	\
Backtick	`

Curly braces	{}
Dot	.
Exclamation mark	!
Hash mark	#
Minus sign or hyphen	-
Parentheses	()
Plus sign	+
Square brackets	[]
Underscore	_

Keyboard keys

To represent keyboard keys, type the tag <kbd> before a key symbol, and then you can or cannot type the closing tag as </kbd>.

Example:

Syntax	Result
`<kbd>Ctrl</kbd>+<kbd>Alt</kbd>+<kbd>Del</kbd>`	`Ctrl+Alt+Del`

Custom Themes

You can change font type and font size, including look and feel of your HTML page by customizing the default theme. For this, you need to see if your Markdown tool allows for this.

Table of Contents

In Markdown, Table of Contents (ToC) is created by using the option given in the Markdown editor you use. ToC is created based on the headings you have in your document.

Alternatively, you can write the syntax for ToC in the same way as you do for backlink, see *Backlink*, page-43.

Type a square bracket [] followed by a parenthesis (). Type the destination in the square bracket and the reference link in the parenthesis. You may also format your ToC in nested list by adding the syntax for unordered list.

Example:

Syntax	Result

*[Sample Heading](#sample heading)
 	
*[Sample Heading](#sample heading)
    *[Heading](##heading)
    *[Heading](##heading)
*[Sample Heading](#sample heading)
 	
*[Sample Heading](#sample heading)
	• Sample Heading
	
	• Sample Heading
	    o Heading
	    o Heading
	
	• Sample Heading
	
	• Sample Heading

Keyboard Shortcuts for Markdown Syntax

Learn Markdown

Learn Keyboard Shortcuts for Syntax

The very purpose of using Markdown is to speed up formatting the text. It is good if you use the keyboard shortcuts for typing various syntaxes.

Following are the shortcuts on your keyboard to type different syntaxes.

Formatting need	Syntax	Shortcut	Result
For bold: type two asterisks	**text**	Ctrl + B	**text**
For italics: type one asterisk	*text*	Ctrl + I	*text*
For bold and italics: type Three asterisks	***text***	Ctrl + B + I	***text***
To underline a term	<u>text</u>	Ctrl + U	text
For strike through: type two tilde marks	~~text~~	Alt + Shift + 5	~~text~~
For regular paragraph	text	Ctrl + 0	text
To insert table		Ctrl + T	

Formatting need	Syntax	Shortcut	Result
For code, type one backtick around the term	`Comment`	Ctrl + Shift + `	`Comment`
For math code	a² — b²	Ctrl + Shift + M	
For block or quote, type one greater than sign	> text	Ctrl + Shift + Q	Text
For link, type one square bracket and one first bracket	[title](http://)	Ctrl + K	Text
For images, type one exclamation, one square bracket, and one first bracket		Ctrl + Shift + I	
For H1, type one asterisk	*Heading 1*	Ctrl + 1	
For H2, type two asterisks	**Heading 2**	Ctrl + 2	
For H3, type three asterisks	***Heading 3***	Ctrl + 3	

Formatting need	Syntax	Shortcut	Result
For H4, type four asterisks	****Heading 4****	Ctrl + 4	
For H5, type five asterisks	*****Heading 5*****	Ctrl + 5	
For H6, type six asterisks	******Heading 6******	Ctrl + 6	
To increase heading level		Ctrl + =	
To decrease heading level		Ctrl + -	
Clear formatting		Ctrl + \	

Printed in Great Britain
by Amazon